Al Fresco Kāma

Al Fresco Kāma

~Love Under the Open Sky~

Alka Pande

SPEAKING TIGER

SPEAKING TIGER BOOKS LLP
125A, Ground Floor, Shahpur Jat, near Asiad Village,
New Delhi 110049

First published by Speaking Tiger Books 2022

ISBN: 978-93-5447-224-4

10 9 8 7 6 5 4 3 2 1

Typeset in Cormorant Garamond by SÜRYA, New Delhi
Printed at : SBM Industries Pvt Ltd, Rai (www.sbmprints.com)

Above: Lady on a swing and her lover in a lush garden. Image from a 19th century illuminated manuscript of the *Kamasutra*.

Page 1: Image from a poster depicting 84 positions for love-making, inspired by the *Kamasutra*. Nathdwara School, 19th century.

Lovers in a garden pavilion at night. Pahari miniature, app. 1760 CE.
National Museum, New Delhi.

~ Introduction ~

I fall on the bed of tender ferns; he lies on my breasts forever.
I embrace him, kiss him; he clings to me, drinking my lips.

[...]

I murmur like a cuckoo; he masters love's secret rite.
My hair is a tangle of wilted flowers; my breasts bear his nail-marks...
Friend, bring Keshi's sublime tormentor to revel with me
I've gone mad waiting for his fickle love to change.

—from Jayadeva's *Gita Govinda*,
translated by Barbara Stoller Miller

The freedom and beauty of the green outdoors—soft beds of grass and ferns; the caress of the breeze; the scent of flowers; birdsong and moonlight—inflame desire in the *nayak* (hero) and the *nayika* (heroine) in ancient and medieval Indian art and literature. And there is no distinction in poetry from that period between romantic and physical desire. Whether the nayak and nayika be mortals or gods, love is always erotic, and its most beautiful expression happens in the lap of nature, as the lovers give themselves to each other without inhibition beneath the open sky.

Krishna's love dances—raas leela—with Radha and the other gopis have been the subject of some of the most beautiful Bhakti poetry, including the works of Jayadeva (12th century CE), Surdas (16th century CE) and Raskhan (16th /17th century CE). In the idyllic semi-wilderness of Vrindavan, on the banks of the Yamuna river, untrammelled passion played out as a cosmic celebration of life. Nidhivan, a forest of sacred Tulsi plants, was the favourite rendezvous of Radha and Krishna, and to this day it is believed that they come here to perform the raas leela every night. No one is allowed into Nidhivan after dark, for the rituals of love should not be disturbed (a lesson that many in India appear to have forgotten).

It is an exceptionally mature civilization that can express the devotee's longing for union with God in the language of human courtship. There is then no shame in love, whether romantic or erotic, and every space, including the outdoors, belongs to lovers by right.

In his *Gita Govinda*, the immortal poetic work on

the love of Radha, a married woman, and the adolescent Krishna, Jayadeva writes:

In spring, when youthful karuna trees look laughing at those who
lose their shame,
When spear-shaped boughs are studding the quarters, piercing
those who are parted from love,
Hari here in the forest dwells, in eager dance with the women folk—

[...]

With his limbs, tender and dark like rows of clumps of blue lotus
flowers,
By herd-girls surrounded—who embrace at pleasure any part of
his body—
Friend, in spring beautiful Hari plays like Kama's own self
Conducting the love sport, with love for all, bringing delight into
*being.**

Innumerable paintings, particularly in the Rajasthani and Pahari miniature tradition, show Krishna in lovely foreplay with the gopis, all of them dancing in forests where the air would have been thick with the heady scent of Champa flowers and creepers of the night blossoming white jasmine.

Eons before Radha and Krishna, Parvati and Shiva were the Prime Couple. All the universe was the theatre

* Translation by George Keyt.

of their desire. The sounds of their passionate lovemaking atop Mount Kailash were heard by the sacred bull Nandi, Shiva's vahana (vehicle) who is also his doorkeeper and trusted companion. Nandi was so moved and awestruck by their divine lovemaking that he not only committed the details to memory, he also whispered them to the celibate sage Vatsyayana. And Vastayana then recorded these and other love acts in 1250 verses. The result was the greatest of all *kama shastras* (erotic texts)—the *Kamasutra*, composed sometime in the 3rd century CE. This Sanskrit classic, translated into every major language of the world, has inspired both men and women to enrich their sexual lives.

~

Kama, or desire, has always been part of the Indian consciousness—one of the four *purusharthas* (stages or goals of life) in Hinduism, the others being dharma (duty, or 'right living'), artha (economic well-being), and moksha (spiritual enlightenment or liberation). Sex is both natural and beautiful and is essential for a good and complete life. It is also sacred. The *Kamasutra* being associated with the primordial divine couple, Shiva and Parvati, its verses were often interpreted in sculptures on the exteriors of temples across India. The gods had no time for hypocrisy.

Among mortals, too, the sexual act was not enjoyed

only in private chambers; lovers did not always retreat indoors and blow out the lamps before they got down to the business of pleasure. The ancient Indian was close to nature, and open spaces, with trees, birds, flowers and other pleasing sights and sensations, would have seemed ideal for lovemaking. Royalty and the otherwise wealthy made love in fragrant gardens, and representations of this lovely indulgence abound in art, the depictions ranging from the exquisite to the playfully absurd (slaying a lion while deep in the act, for instance).

As we scroll through the pages of the *kama shastras*, the outdoors find numerous mentions. Classical Sanskrit literature is replete with such references. There are lush gardens and forests of enchantment where animals respond to each other's mating calls, and the cooling moon and monsoon clouds stoke the fires of lust. In these fecund and sacred patches of earth bursting with nature's bounty, lovers seek erotic delight with breathtaking abandon.

This verdant, shaded ambience was perfect for lovemaking during the hot Indian summers. The love bowers were very thoughtfully situated in isolated corners of the palace and public gardens. The fragrant shrubs and creepers heightened the intensity of the lovers' passion.

The art and architecture of pre-modern India, particularly of the upper classes, were marked by unapologetic opulence and eroticism. Vatsyayana mentions aesthetic love chambers in the yard or garden of the nagaraka, the man about town, where his mistresses and courtesans were invited. In Sanskrit poetry, the *dolagriha*, the garden space with a swing, is best suited for refined and unhurried rituals of pleasure.

The town garden, known as *nagaropavana*, was the ideal setting for lovers' trysts. It features prominently in the work of the pre-eminent Sanskrit poet Kalidasa ($4^{th}/5^{th}$ century CE). His *nagaropavana* is elaborately laid out, with water tanks, arbours of flowering creepers, swings and stone benches, and posts for tame peacocks. In his epic poem *Raghuvamsam*, the royal couple Aja and Indumati make love in a garden which is adorned with special pavilions for love sports. Another king has sexual encounters with his female attendants in a verdant bower.

Manasollasa (literally, 'Delighter of the Mind'), a 12th-century encyclopaedic treatise from southern India, describes, with reference to Kalidasa, a secret chamber called *gudhamohanagriha*. It was constructed in a garden at the level of water, like a sunken courtyard or basement, and was meant for *kamabhoga*, or 'carnal pleasure'.

In the play *Svapnavasavadattam*, by one of India's earliest playwrights, Bhasa (3rd or 2nd century BCE), there is mention of painted wooden pavilions with paintings of birds and bees setting the mood for love. There are also temporary chambers made with plantain leaves for couples to have sex in. A charming novelty! But an even greater novelty is described in the 11th-century poet Bilhana's long poem *Vikramankadevacharita*—an erotic sport in which women in the palace of King Vikramanka swing from one creeper to another like trapeze artists.

The *Dasakumaracharita* by Dandin (7th century CE) has beautiful descriptions of a *samketagriha*, a meeting place for lovers in a public garden with beautiful pavilions constructed with fragrant creepers, and doorways made of red Asoka branches. Here, aphrodisiacs, ornate ivory fans, bowls with scented water and betel nut were kept for the lovers to sharpen their senses and heighten their pleasure.

Some literary records show that in the royal landscape of Central India, from Orchha to Silhara to the Durvasa caves, there were many *aramampavate* or pleasure houses on top of natural hills. Elsewhere, there were *kridaparvats*, artificially made hills where royalty conducted elaborate sexual games, often on jewelled benches. The poet and prose writer Banabhatta (7th century CE) describes a *kridaparvat* which was a mansion full of mirrors where the lovers could watch themselves in the sexual act.

The external façade of several such structures was embellished with animal motifs: *gajasimha*, a lion with an elephant head; *udyatsimha*, prancing lions; *sukasarika*, parrots or myna birds; *sarasa*, cranes or herons; *hamsa*, the royal goose or swan. These animals were typical to the structural element of the pleasure pavilions because each animal possessed an erotic symbolism: the grace and voluptuous girth of the elephant, the sensuality and fidelity of the swan, the ferocious vigour of the lion, and so on.

Flowers, too, were central to the vocabulary of passion. The bow of Kamadeva, the god of erotic love, is made of vines and fragrant flowers. With this bow he shoots arrows of desire which are also tipped with flowers. The flowers on Kama's arrows are aravinda (white lotus), asoka, cuta (mango flower), navamallika (jasmine) and nilotpala (blue lotus). They evoke the sensations of *unmada* (infatuation), *tapana* (excitement), *soshana* (parching or withering), *stambhana* (heating) and *sammohana* (hypnosis)—the different stages of passion.

If green and verdant spaces were essential for erotic bliss in the tropical climate of the Indian subcontinent, so was water. Radha, Krishna and the gopis were never far from the Yamuna; in fact, they were often at play in its waters. Wealthy mortals brought the waters to their theatres of pleasure—there were fountains, water tanks and water channels in their gardens, terraces and garden pavilions. Such was the sophistication that the amorous play we see in Hollywood's bathtubs appears hopelessly contrived in comparison. There was the *dharagriha*, or chamber with water fountains, described in literary Sanskrit texts like Bilahana's *Vikramankadevacharita*. And water tanks edged with seductive floral carvings that appear in classical Buddhist texts like *Digha Nikaya*. Or the *kelisaras*, a pond for love sports mentioned in inscriptions on the walls of temples in Khajuraho.

Many illuminated manuscripts of *kama shastras* like the *Kamasutra*, *Anangaranga*, *Amrushatakam*, *Rati Rahasya* and private pleasure albums show lovers in *jalakrida*, love-play in ponds and tanks. These artificial water bodies are generally packed with beautiful lotuses and aquatic wildlife. Peacocks drinking from the ponds and ducks and swans swimming in them add to the sensuality.

These depictions and descriptions have inspired our cinema, and many a heroine in a thin white sari has danced under a waterfall with her hero. But alas, the sensuality has been missing and the enjoyment has rarely been hers. Our cinema has yet to learn the art of kama. It could take a closer look at the images reproduced in the pages that follow.

ALKA PANDE
Vasant, 2022

Divine love in the lap of nature. Pahari miniature, 18th century. Rietberg Museum, Zurich.

Prince Murad, son of Akbar, with his wife Mirza in a garden. Mughal School, 16th century. Freer Gallery of Art.

Prince and his consort in a palace veranda. Painting on ivory in the Mughal style, early 20th century. Collection of Beroze and Michel Sabatier, La Rochelle.

Lady urges patience. Rajasthan, 20th century. Private collection.

Lovers on chairs on the terrace. Jodhpur School, late 19th century. Private collection.

Opposite and above: **Leisurely love in springtime, while a tame peacock looks on. Jodhpur School, close of the 19th century. Private collection.**

Indulgence. Jaipur School, app. 1880. Private collection.

Timid princess and patient prince. Painting on ivory, 19th century.
Collection of the Museum of Erotics and Mythology, Brussels.

Opposite and above: Two moments of passion on a terrace. Jaipur School, app. 1880. Private collection.

Above: The hills are alive with the sound of love. Rajasthan, late 19th century. Private collection.

Opposite: Raja on his terrace. Kota School, 1870. Source: Wikipedia.

Prince and lady on terrace at night. Rajasthan, app. 1790.
Private collection.

The nagarika's garden pavilion. Malwa School, 1675-1700.
Walters Art Museum.

An outdoor lovers' pavilion with a fountain. Sirohi School, early 19th century. Private collection.

Poolside love-making. Chamba School, app. 1700 CE.
Walters Art Museum.

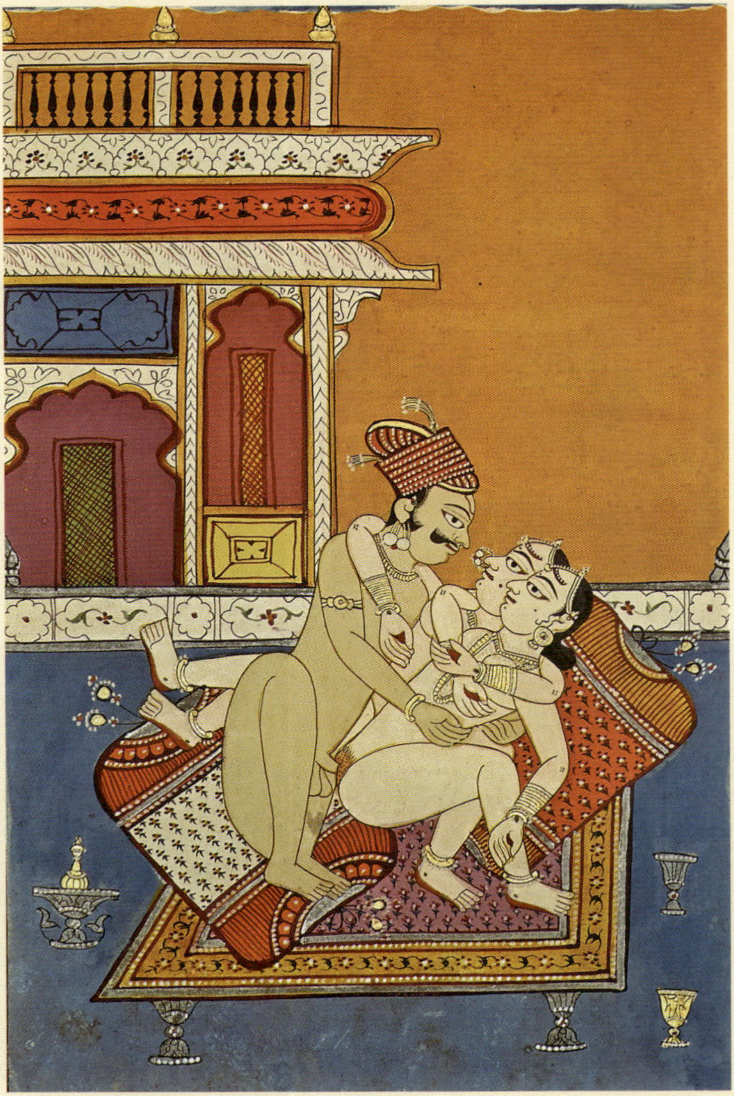

Threesome on a terrace. Jodhpur School, 19th century.
Private collection.

The courtesan and the firangi. Jaipur School, late 19th century. Private collection.

Above and opposite: Rituals of unhurried love. Erotic paintings of the Jodhpur School from the close of the 19th century. Private collection.

Above and opposite: Further rituals of unhurried love. Erotic paintings of the Jodhpur School from the close of the 19th century. Private collection.

Opposite and above: Bold lover and the shy one. Jaipur School, late 19th or early 20th century. Private collection.

Above and opposite: Gardens of love. Orchha School, app. 1800.
Private collection.

Opposite and above: Love and other arts. Orchha School, app. 1800. Private collection.

The wine of love. Painting on ivory, early 20th century. Museum of Erotics and Mythology, Brussels.

The wheel of love. Painting on ivory, early 20th century. Museum of Erotics and Mythology, Brussels.

Above: A conversation. Painting from a pleasure album produced in the late 19th century. Nathdwara School. Private collection.

Opposite: The royal couple in their pleasure yard. Painting on ivory, late 19th or early 20th century. Museum of Erotics and Mythology, Brussels.

Above and opposite: No beast shall interrupt the rituals of love in the wilderness. Nathdwara School, close of the 19th century. Private collection.

Making love in the hot afternoon in a terrace garden cooled by water fountains. Deccan School, 1760 CE. Private collection.

On the riverbank, with swans as witness. Painting from an Urdu adaptation of the *Kamasutra*. Possibly early 20th century.

The lovers Sohni and Mahiwal meet for a night of love by the river. Bundi School, app. 1800 CE. Rietberg Museum, Zurich.

The erotic and the sacred co-exist. Two gopis sport in the river, while a holy vision unfolds in a tree behind them. Seventeenth-century Indian miniature in the collection of the Brooklyn Museum.

Above: Lovers on a terrace with attendants. Unfinished painting of the Deccan School, 19th century. Private collection.

Opposite: Man with three women. Unfinished colour sketch from Rajasthan, end of the 19th century. Collection of Beroze and Michel Sabatier, La Rochelle.

Lovers confront a leopard. Painting from a series inspired by the Sufi text Madhu-Malati. Pahari miniature from Kulu, 1810 CE. Reitberg Museum, Zurich.

At the edge of a garden. Mid- or late 19th century, Northwest India.

Pleasuring her on a garden bench. Nathdwara, 19th century. From a poster of 84 sex positions in a private collection in Ahmedabad. (Images on pages 61-63 also from the same poster.)

Pointing to the moon that lights up their act of love.
Nathdwara School.

Lady with her lover and her pet. Nathdwara School.

Swing time. Nathdwara School.

Up on a tree on a full-moon night. Nathdwara School.

Above: Lovers oblivious to clouds building up on the horizon, promising rain. Jaipur School, late 19th century.

Opposite: Two lovers in embrace, using carrots as dildos. Painting from an Indian erotic manuscript in Persian; 19th century. Wellcome Library.

Holy men and a woman in a bisexual foursome. Source: Wikimedia Commons.

Three lovers and some curious animals. Sketch on paper; Rajasthan, 19th century. Collection of Beroze and Michel Sabatier, La Rochelle.

Above: The stars rain down their light on love.

Opposite: Nature provides a soft bed for love.

Both paintings from the Nathdwara School, 19th century. Private collection.

Alka Pande trained as an art historian and has written prolifically on Indology and Art History. She is the author of several books with a special interest in gender and sexuality; her PhD thesis was on the theme of Ardhanarishvara. She has written extensively on erotic Indian literature and art as well. Her books include *Masterpieces of Indian Art*; *Shringara: The Many Faces of Indian Beauty*; *Body Sutra: Tracing the Human Form Through Art & Imagination*; *The New Age Kamasutra for Women* and *Pha(bu)llus: A Cultural History*.

Alka Pande was awarded the Chevalier dans l'Ordre des Arts et des Lettres in 2006 by the French government.